First published 1998

Published by Wooden Books Ltd.
Walkmill, Cascob, Presteigne, Powys, Wales LD8 2NT

British Library Cataloguing in Publication Data
Rhys, J.
A Birth of Taliesin

A CIP catalogue record for this book is
available from the British Library

ISBN 1 902418 01 8

Printed in Great Britain
by Redwood Books Ltd,
Trowbridge, Wiltshire, UK.

WOODEN BOOKS

A BIRTH OF TALIESIN

an old story from Glasynys
put into the English by

Sir John Rhys

with illustrations by

Caroline Wallis

This short story appears in translation in an article by Sir John Rhys in the 1882 Journal of the Honourable Society of Cymmrodorion. He quotes as his source an article by Glasynys in 'Cymru Fu' , a periodical of the time. The story is reproduced here with the kind permission and help of the Society. Some small changes have been made for today's tongue.

Glasynys, 'Blue Isle', was the bardic name of Owen Wyne Jones, born in Caernshire in 1828. A novelist and poet, he also spent time collecting the ghost and fairy stories of pre-Methodist Wales.

Sir John Rees was born at midsummer in 1840 in Cardiganshire. One of the foremost Celtic scholars of his day his studies ranged from ancient stone inscriptions to Welsh and Manx folk and fairy lore. A philologist, metrologist, linguist and Arthurian scholar he began the Celtic chair at Jesus College, Oxford, and was knighted in 1907.

Taliesin was a Welsh poet of the sixth century AD, when the Welsh language was emerging from the Brythonic. Poems attributed to Taliesin appear in the thirteenth century 'Book of Taliesin', one of a few early manuscripts containing pre-Norman Welsh verse. The bard has also been connected with the shadowy figure of the Arthurian Merlin.

A BIRTH OF
TALIESIN

ONCE upon a time a shepherd-boy had gone up a mountain. That day, like many before and after, was exceedingly misty.

Now, though he was very well acquainted with the place he lost his way, and walked backwards and forwards for many a long hour.

At last he got into a low rushy spot, where he saw before him many circular rings.

He at once recalled the place, and began to fear the worst. He had heard, many hundreds of times, of the bitter experiences in those rings of many a shepherd who had happened to chance on the dancing place or the circles of the Fair Family.

He hastened away as far as ever he could, lest he should be ruined like the rest; but, though he exerted himself to the point of perspiring and losing his breath, there he was, and there he continued to be ...

... a long time.

AT last he was met by a little fat old man, with merry blue eyes, who asked him what he was doing.

He answered that he was trying to find his way homewards.

"Oh", said he.

"Come after me, and do not utter a word until I bid thee."

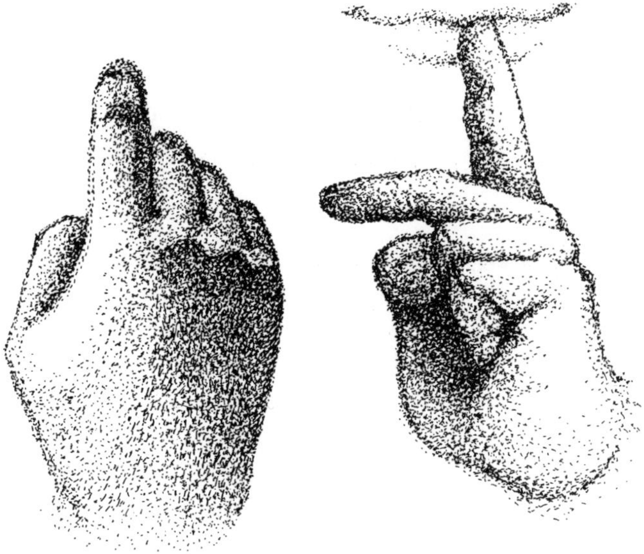

This the shepherd-boy did, following him on and on until they came to an oval stone;

and the little old fat man lifted it, after tapping the middle of it, three times, with his walking stick.

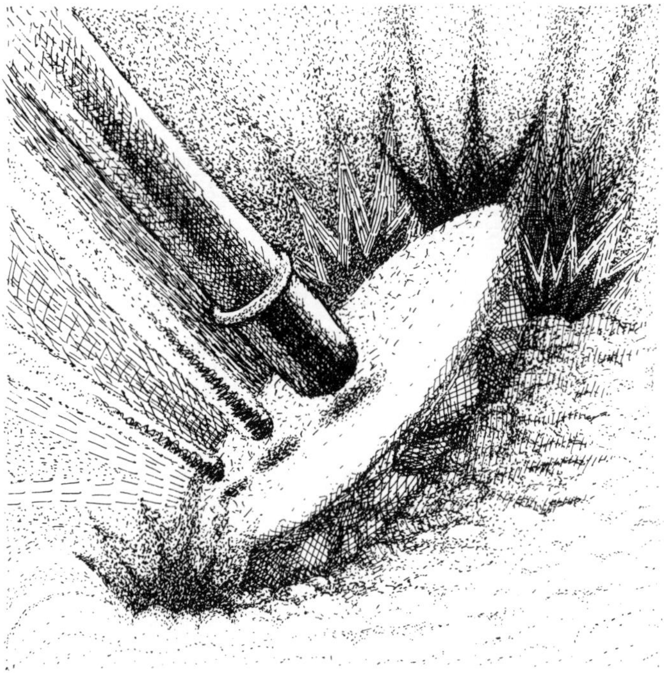

There was a narrow path with
stairs to be seen here and there;

- and a sort of whitish light,
inclining grey to blue, was to be
seen radiating from the stones.

"Follow me fearlessly,"
said the little fat man;
"No harm will be done thee."

So the poor youth went ...
as reluctantly as a dog
to be hanged.

BUT presently a fine, wooded, fertile country spread itself out before them, with well-arranged mansions dotting it over, while every kind of apparent magnificence met the eye and seemed to smile in its landscape;

The bright waters of its rivers meandered in twisted streams, and its hills were covered with the luxuriant verdure of their grassy growth, and the mountains with a glossy fleece of smooth pasture.

By the time they had reached the stout gentleman's mansion, the young man's senses had been bewildered by the sweet cadence of the music which the birds poured forth from the groves;

Then there was gold there to dazzle his eyes, and silver flashing on his sight.

He saw there all kinds of
musical instruments and all
sorts of things for playing;

but he could discern no
inhabitant in the whole place.

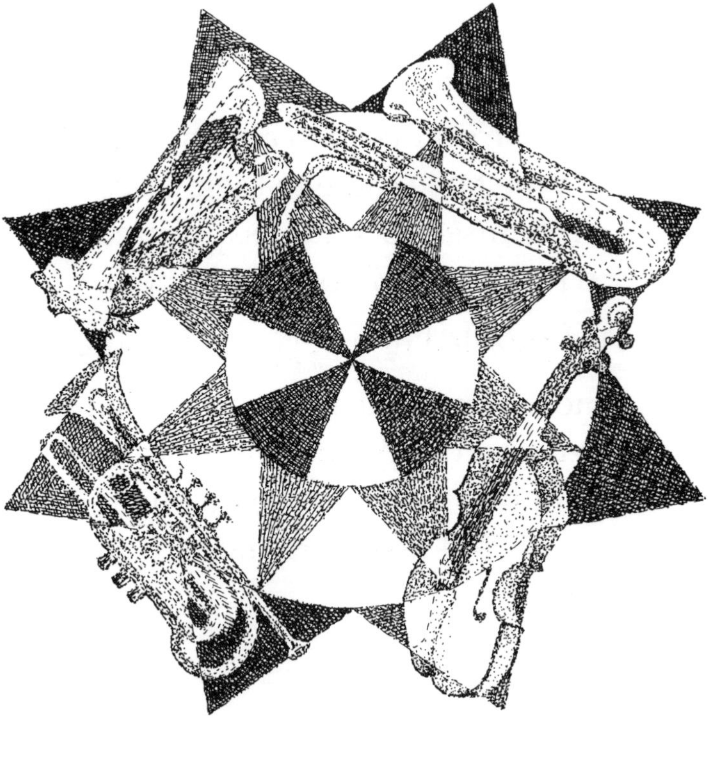

When he sat down to eat, the dishes on the table came to their place of themselves, and disappeared when one had done with them.

This puzzled him beyond measure.

... moreover, he heard people talking together around him, but for the life of him he could see no one but his old friend.

AT length the fat man said to him:
"Thou canst now talk as much as it may please thee."

But when he attempted to move his tongue, it would no more stir than if it had been a lump of ice, which greatly frightened him.

At this point, a fine old lady, with health and benevolence shining in her face, came to them and slightly smiled at the shepherd.

The mother was followed by her three daughters, who were remarkably beautiful. They gazed with somewhat playful looks at him, and at length began to talk to him;

... but his tongue would not wag.

Then one of the girls came to him, and, playing with his yellow and curly locks, gave him a smart kiss on his ruddy lips.

This loosened the string that bound his tongue, and he began to talk freely and eloquently.

THERE he was, under
the charm of that kiss,
in the bliss of happiness;
and there he remained a year
and a day - without knowing
that he had passed more than
a day among them;

... for he had got into a country
where there was no reckoning
of time.

But by and by he began to feel somewhat of a longing to visit his old home, and asked the stout old man if he might go.

"Stay a little yet," said he, "and thou shalt go for a while."

That passed: he stayed on; but Olwen, for that was the name of the damsel that had kissed him, was very unwilling that he should depart. She looked sad every time he talked of going away; nor was he himself without feeling a sort of a cold thrill passing through him at the thought of leaving her.

On condition, however, of returning, he obtained leave to go, provided with plenty of gold and silver, of trinkets and gems.

WHEN he reached home, nobody knew who he was; it had been the belief that he had been killed by another shepherd, who had then run far away to America.

But here was Einion Las at home, and everyone wondered to see that the shepherd boy had got to look like a wealthy man: His manners, his dress, his language, and the treasure he had with him - all conspired to give him the air of a gentleman.

He went back one Thursday night, the first of the moon that month, as suddenly as he had left the first time...

... and nobody knew whither.

There was great joy in the country below when Einion returned thither, and nobody was more rejoiced at it than Olwen, his beloved.

The two were right impatient to get married; but it was necessary to do that quietly, for the Family below hated nothing more than fuss and noise.

So, in a sort of a half secret fashion, they were wedded.

Einion was very desirous to go once more amongst his own people, accompanied, to be sure, by his wife.

After he had long been entreating the old man for leave, they set out on two white ponies that were, in fact, more like snow than anything else in point of colour.

SO, he arrived with his consort in his old home, and it was the opinion of all that Einion's wife was the handsomest person they had anywhere seen.

Whilst at home, a son was born
to them, to whom they
gave the name of
Taliesin.

Einion was now in the enjoyment of high repute, and his wife received proper respect. Their wealth was immense, and soon they acquired a large estate;

But it was not long till people began to inquire after the pedigree of Einion's wife - the country was of the opinion that it was not the right thing to be without pedigree.

Einion was questioned about it, without his giving any satisfactory answer, and it was concluded that she was one of the Fair Family.

"Certainly", replied Einion.

"There can be no doubt that she comes from a very fair family; for she has two sisters who are as fair as she, and, if you saw them together you would admit that name to be a capital one."

This, then, is the reason why the remarkable family in the land of Charm and Phantasy are called the Fair Family.